THE HARD HOURS

THE
HARD HOURS

POEMS BY

ANTHONY HECHT

Were is that lawhing and that song,
That trayling and that proude gong,
Tho havekes and tho houndes?
Al that joye is went away,
That wele is comen to weylaway,
To manye harde stoundes.

Atheneum   *New York   1967*

CLAIR DE LUNE, A HILL *and* A LETTER *were originally published in* THE NEW YORKER; TARANTULA *was originally published in* POETRY; *other poems appeared originally in Book Week, Botteghe Oscure, Harper's Bazaar, Hudson Review, Kenyon Review, The Nation, The Noble Savage, Partisan Review, Quarterly Review of Literature, Transatlantic Review, and Voices:* THE SEVEN DEADLY SINS *and* IMPROVISATIONS ON AESOP *were originally published by The Gehenna Press, with wood engravings by Leonard Baskin*

Library of Congress catalog card number 67–25474
Published simultaneously in Canada by McClelland and Stewart Ltd.
Composed and printed by Clarke and Way, New York
Bound by H. Wolff, New York
Designed by Harry Ford
First Edition

For my sons

JASON *and* ADAM

CONTENTS

From A SUMMONING OF STONES (1954)

THE HARD HOURS

A HILL

In Italy, where this sort of thing can occur,
I had a vision once—though you understand
It was nothing at all like Dante's, or the visions of saints,
And perhaps not a vision at all. I was with some friends,
Picking my way through a warm sunlit piazza
In the early morning. A clear fretwork of shadows
From huge umbrellas littered the pavement and made
A sort of lucent shallows in which was moored
A small navy of carts. Books, coins, old maps,
Cheap landscapes and ugly religious prints
Were all on sale. The colors and noise
Like the flying hands were gestures of exultation,
So that even the bargaining
Rose to the ear like a voluble godliness.
And then, when it happened, the noises suddenly stopped,
And it got darker; pushcarts and people dissolved
And even the great Farnese Palace itself
Was gone, for all its marble; in its place
Was a hill, mole-colored and bare. It was very cold,
Close to freezing, with a promise of snow.
The trees were like old ironwork gathered for scrap
Outside a factory wall. There was no wind,
And the only sound for a while was the little click
Of ice as it broke in the mud under my feet.
I saw a piece of ribbon snagged on a hedge,
But no other sign of life. And then I heard
What seemed the crack of a rifle. A hunter, I guessed;
At least I was not alone. But just after that
Came the soft and papery crash
Of a great branch somewhere unseen falling to earth.

And that was all, except for the cold and silence
That promised to last forever, like the hill.

Then prices came through, and fingers, and I was restored
To the sunlight and my friends. But for more than a week

I was scared by the plain bitterness of what I had seen.
All this happened about ten years ago,
And it hasn't troubled me since, but at last, today,
I remembered that hill; it lies just to the left
Of the road north of Poughkeepsie; and as a boy
I stood before it for hours in wintertime.

THIRD AVENUE IN SUNLIGHT

Third Avenue in sunlight. Nature's error.
Already the bars are filled and John is there.
Beneath a plentiful lady over the mirror
He tilts his glass in the mild mahogany air.

I think of him when he first got out of college,
Serious, thin, unlikely to succeed;
For several months he hung around the Village,
Boldly T-shirted, unfettered but unfreed.

Now he confides to a stranger, "I was first scout,
And kept my glimmers peeled till after dark.
Our outfit had as its sign a bloody knout,
We met behind the museum in Central Park.

Of course, we were kids." But still those savages,
War-painted, a flap of leather at the loins,
File silently against him. Hostages
Are never taken. One summer, in Des Moines,

They entered his hotel room, tomahawks
Flashing like barracuda. He tried to pray.
Three years of treatment. Occasionally he talks
About how he almost didn't get away.

Daily the prowling sunlight whets its knife
Along the sidewalk. We almost never meet.
In the Rembrandt dark he lifts his amber life.
My bar is somewhat further down the street.

TARANTULA or THE DANCE OF DEATH

During the plague I came into my own.
It was a time of smoke-pots in the house
Against infection. The blind head of bone
         Grinned its abuse

Like a good democrat at everyone.
Runes were recited daily, charms were applied.
That was the time I came into my own.
         Half Europe died.

The symptoms are a fever and dark spots
First on the hands, then on the face and neck,
But even before the body, the mind rots.
         You can be sick

Only a day with it before you're dead.
But the most curious part of it is the dance.
The victim goes, in short, out of his head.
         A sort of trance

Glazes the eyes, and then the muscles take
His will away from him, the legs begin
Their funeral jig, the arms and belly shake
         Like souls in sin.

Some, caught in these convulsions, have been known
To fall from windows, fracturing the spine.
Others have drowned in streams. The smooth head-stone,
         The box of pine,

Are not for the likes of these. Moreover, flame
Is powerless against contagion.
That was the black winter when I came
         Into my own.

THE END OF THE WEEKEND

A dying firelight slides along the quirt
Of the cast-iron cowboy where he leans
Against my father's books. The lariat
Whirls into darkness. My girl, in skin-tight jeans,
Fingers a page of Captain Marryat,
Inviting insolent shadows to her shirt.

We rise together to the second floor.
Outside, across the lake, an endless wind
Whips at the headstones of the dead and wails
In the trees for all who have and have not sinned.
She rubs against me and I feel her nails.
Although we are alone, I lock the door.

The eventual shapes of all our formless prayers,
This dark, this cabin of loose imaginings,
Wind, lake, lip, everything awaits
The slow unloosening of her underthings.
And then the noise. Something is dropped. It grates
Against the attic beams.
                              I climb the stairs,

Armed with a belt.
                              A long magnesium strip
Of moonlight from the dormer cuts a path
Among the shattered skeletons of mice.
A great black presence beats its wings in wrath.
Above the boneyard burn its golden eyes.
Some small grey fur is pulsing in its grip.

MESSAGE FROM THE CITY

It is raining here.
On my neighbor's fire escape
geraniums are set out
in their brick-clay pots,
along with the mop,
old dishrags, and a cracked
enamel bowl for the dog.

I think of you out there
on the sandy edge of things,
rain strafing the beach,
the white maturity
of bones and broken shells,
and little tin shovels and cars
rusting under the house.

And between us there is—what?
Love and constraint,
conditions, conditions,
and several hundred miles
of billboards, filling-stations,
and little dripping gardens.
The fir tree full of whispers,
trinkets of water,
the bob, duck, and release
of the weighted rose,
life in the freshened stones.
(They used to say that rain
is good for growing boys,
and once I stood out in it
hoping to rise a foot.
The biggest drops fattened
on the gutters under the eaves,
sidled along the slant,
picked up speed, let go,
and met their dooms in a "plock"

beside my gleaming shins.
I must have been near the size
of your older son.)

Yesterday was nice.
I took my boys to the park.
We played Ogre on the grass.
I am, of course, the Ogre,
and invariably get killed.
Merciless and barefooted,
they sneak up from behind
and they let me have it.

O my dear, my dear,
today the rain pummels
the sour geraniums
and darkens the grey pilings
of your house, built upon sand.
And both of us, full grown,
have weathered a long year.
Perhaps your casual glance
will settle from time to time
on the sea's travelling muscles
that flex and roll their strength
under its rain-pocked skin.
And will see where the salt winds
have blown bare the seaward side
of the berry bushes,
and will notice
the faint, fresh
smell of iodine.

JASON

And from America the golden fleece   MARLOWE

The room is full of gold.
Is it a chapel? Is that the genuine buzz
Of cherubim, the wingèd goods?
Is it no more than sun that floods
To pool itself at her uncovered breast?
O lights, o numina, behold
How we are gifted. He who never was,
Is, and her fingers bless him and are blessed.

That blessedness is tossed
In a wild, dodging light. Suddenly clear
And poised in heavenly desire
Prophets and eastern saints take fire
And fuse with gold in windows across the way,
And turn to liquid, and are lost.
And now there deepens over lakes of air
A remembered stillness of the seventh day

Borne in on the soft cruise
And sway of birds. Slowly the ancient seas,
Those black, predestined waters rise
Lisping and calm before my eyes,
And Massachusetts rises out of foam
A state of mind in which by twos
All beasts browse among barns and apple trees
As in their earliest peace, and the dove comes home.

Tonight, my dear, when the moon
Settles the radiant dust of every man,
Powders the bedsheets and the floor
With lightness of those gone before,
Sleep then, and dream the story as foretold:
Dream how a little boy alone
With a wooden sword and the top of a garbage can
Triumphs in gardens full of marigold.

9

BEHOLD THE LILIES OF THE FIELD

for Leonard Baskin

And now. An attempt.
Don't tense yourself; take it easy.
Look at the flowers there in the glass bowl.
Yes, they are lovely and fresh. I remember
Giving my mother flowers once, rather like those
(Are they narcissus or jonquils?)
And I hoped she would show some pleasure in them
But got that mechanical enthusiastic show
She used on the telephone once in praising some friend
For thoughtfulness or good taste or whatever it was,
And when she hung up, turned to us all and said,
"God, what a bore she is!"
I think she was trying to show us how honest she was,
At least with us. But the effect
Was just the opposite, and now I don't think
She knows what honesty is. "Your mother's a whore,"
Someone said, not meaning she slept around,
Though perhaps this was part of it, but
Meaning she had lost all sense of honor,
And I think this is true.

But that's not what I wanted to say.
What was it I wanted to say?
When he said that about Mother, I had to laugh,
I really did, it was so amazingly true.
Where was I?
Lie back. Relax.
Oh yes. I remember now what it was.
It was what I saw them do to the emperor.
They captured him, you know. Eagles and all.
They stripped him, and made an iron collar for his neck,
And they made a cage out of our captured spears,
And they put him inside, naked and collared,
And exposed to the view of the whole enemy camp.
And I was tied to a post and made to watch

When he was taken out and flogged by one of their generals
And then forced to offer his ripped back
As a mounting block for the barbarian king
To get on his horse;
And one time to get down on all fours to be the royal throne
When the king received our ambassadors
To discuss the question of ransom.
Of course, he didn't want ransom.
And I was tied to a post and made to watch.
That's enough for now. Lie back. Try to relax.
No, that's not all.
They kept it up for two months.
We were taken to their outmost provinces.
It was always the same, and we were always made to watch,
The others and I. How he stood it, I don't know.
And then suddenly
There were no more floggings or humiliations,
The king's personal doctor saw to his back,
He was given decent clothing, and the collar was taken off,
And they treated us all with a special courtesy.
By the time we reached their capital city
His back was completely healed.
They had taken the cage apart—
But of course they didn't give us back our spears.
Then later that month, it was a warm afternoon in May,
The rest of us were marched out to the central square.
The crowds were there already, and the posts were set up,
To which we were tied in the old watching positions.
And he was brought out in the old way, and stripped,
And then tied flat on a big rectangular table
So that only his head could move.
Then the king made a short speech to the crowds,
To which they responded with gasps of wild excitement,
And which was then translated for the rest of us.
It was the sentence. He was to be flayed alive,
As slowly as possible, to drag out the pain.
And we were made to watch. The king's personal doctor,

The one who had tended his back,
Came forward with a tray of surgical knives.
They began at the feet.
And we were not allowed to close our eyes
Or to look away. When they were done, hours later,
The skin was turned over to one of their saddle-makers
To be tanned and stuffed and sewn. And for what?
A hideous life-sized doll, filled out with straw,
In the skin of the Roman Emperor, Valerian,
With blanks of mother-of-pearl under the eyelids,
And painted shells that had been prepared beforehand
For the fingernails and toenails,
Roughly cross-stitched on the inseam of the legs
And up the back to the center of the head,
Swung in the wind on a rope from the palace flag-pole;
And young girls were brought there by their mothers
To be told about the male anatomy.
His death had taken hours.
They were very patient.
And with him passed away the honor of Rome.

In the end, I was ransomed. Mother paid for me.
You must rest now. You must. Lean back.
Look at the flowers.
Yes. I am looking. I wish I could be like them.

PIG

In the manger of course were cows and the Child Himself
        Was like unto a lamb
Who should come in the fulness of time on an ass's back
        Into Jerusalem

And all things be redeemed—the suckling babe
        Lie safe in the serpent's home
And the lion eat straw like the ox and roar its love
        to Mark and to Jerome

And God's Peaceable Kingdom return among them all
        Save one full of offense
Into which the thousand fiends of a human soul
        Were cast and driven hence

And the one thus cured gone up into the hills
        To worship and to pray:
O Swine that takest away our sins
        That takest away

OSTIA ANTICA

for William and Dale MacDonald

Given this light,
The departing thunderhead in its anger
Off to one side, and given
These ancient stones in their setting, themselves refreshed
And rendered strangely younger
By wetness alive with the wriggling brass of heaven,
Where is the spirit's part unwashed
Of all poor spite?

The cypress thrust,
Greened in the glass of air as never
Since the first greenness offered,
Not to desire our prayer: "To ghostly creatures,
Peace, and an end of fever
Till all this dust assemble," but delivered
To their resistless lives and natures,
Rise as they must.

And the broken wall
Is only itself, deeply accepting
The sun's warmth to its bricks.
The puddles blink; a snail marches the Roman
Road of its own adopting.
The marble nymph is stripped to the flush of sex
As if in truth this timeless, human
Instant were all.

Is it the bird's
Voice, the delicious voice of water,
Addresses us on the splendid
Topic of love? And promises to youth
Still livelier forms and whiter?
Here are quick freshes, here is the body suspended
In its firm blessing, here the mouth
Finds out its words.

See, they arise
In the sign of ivy, the young males
To their strength, the meadows restored;
Concupiscence of eye, and the world's pride;
Of love, the naked skills.
At the pool's edge, the rippled image cleared,
That face set among leaves is glad,
Noble and wise.

What was begun,
The mastered force, breeds and is healing.
Pebbles and clover speak.
Each hanging waterdrop burns with a fierce
Bead of the sun's instilling.
But softly, beneath the flutesong and volatile shriek
Of birds, are to be heard discourse
Mother and son.

"If there were hushed
To us the images of earth, its poles
Hushed, and the waters of it,
And hushed the tumult of the flesh, even
The voice intrinsic of our souls,
Each tongue and token hushed and the long habit
Of thought, if that first light, the given
To us were hushed,

So that the washed
Object, fixed in the sun, were dumb,
And to the mind its brilliance
Were from beyond itself, and the mind were clear
As the unclouded dome
Wherein all things diminish, in that silence
Might we not confidently hear
God as he wished?"

Ostia Antica

Then from the grove
Suddenly falls a flight of bells.
A figure moves from the wood,
Darkly approaching at the hour of vespers
Along the ruined walls.
And bearing heavy articles of blood
And symbols of endurance, whispers,
"This is love."

THE DOVER BITCH *A Criticism of Life*

for Andrews Wanning

So there stood Matthew Arnold and this girl
With the cliffs of England crumbling away behind them,
And he said to her, "Try to be true to me,
And I'll do the same for you, for things are bad
All over, etc., etc."
Well now, I knew this girl. It's true she had read
Sophocles in a fairly good translation
And caught that bitter allusion to the sea,
But all the time he was talking she had in mind
The notion of what his whiskers would feel like
On the back of her neck. She told me later on
That after a while she got to looking out
At the lights across the channel, and really felt sad,
Thinking of all the wine and enormous beds
And blandishments in French and the perfumes.
And then she got really angry. To have been brought
All the way down from London, and then be addressed
As a sort of mournful cosmic last resort
Is really tough on a girl, and she was pretty.
Anyway, she watched him pace the room
And finger his watch-chain and seem to sweat a bit,
And then she said one or two unprintable things.
But you mustn't judge her by that. What I mean to say is,
She's really all right. I still see her once in a while
And she always treats me right. We have a drink
And I give her a good time, and perhaps it's a year
Before I see her again, but there she is,
Running to fat, but dependable as they come.
And sometimes I bring her a bottle of *Nuit d'Amour*.

TO A MADONNA *Ex-Voto in the Spanish Style*

for Allen Tate

Madonna, mistress, I shall build for you
An altar of my misery, and hew
Out of my heart's remote and midnight pitch,
Far from all worldly lusts and sneers, a niche
Enamelled totally in gold and blue
Where I shall set you up and worship you.
And of my verse, like hammered silver lace
Studded with amethysts of rhyme, I'll place
A hand-wrought crown upon your head, and I'll
Make you a coat in the barbaric style,
Picked out in seedling tears instead of pearl,
That you shall wear like mail, my mortal girl,
Lined with suspicion, made of jealousy,
Encasing all your charms, that none may see.
As for the intimate part of your attire,
Your dress shall be composed of my desire,
Rising and falling, swirling from your knees
To your round hills and deep declivities.
Of the respect I owe you I shall make
A pair of satin shoes that they may take—
Though most unworthily prepared to do it—
The authentic shape and imprint of your foot.
And if I fail, for all my proffered boon,
To make a silver footstool of the moon,
Victorious queen, I place beneath your heel
The head of this black serpent that I feel
Gnawing at my intestines all the time,
Swollen with hate and venomous with crime.
You shall behold my thoughts like tapers lit
Before your flowered shrine, and brightening it,
Reflected in the semi-dome's clear skies
Like so many fierce stars or fiery eyes.
And I shall be as myrrh and frankincense,
Rising forever in a smoky trance,
And the dark cloud of my tormented hopes

Shall lift in yearning toward your snowy slopes.
And finally, to render you more real,
I shall make seven blades of Spanish steel
Out of the Seven Deadly Sins, and I
Shall mix my love with murderous savagery,
And like a circus knife-thrower, I'll aim
At the pure center of your gentle frame,
And plunge those blades into your beating heart,
Your bleeding, suffering, palpitating heart.

(AFTER BAUDELAIRE)

CLAIR DE LUNE

Powder and scent and silence. The young dwarf
Shoulders his lute. The moon is Levantine.
It settles its pearl in every glass of wine.
Harlequin is already at the wharf.

The gallant is masked. A pressure of his thumb
Communicates cutaneous interest.
On the smooth upward swelling of a breast
A small black heart is fixed with spirit gum.

The thieving moment is now. Deftly, Pierrot
Exits, bearing a tray of fruits and coins.
A monkey, chained by his tiny loins,
Is taken aboard. They let their moorings go.

Silence. Even the god shall soon be gone.
Shadows, in their cool, tidal enterprise,
Have eaten away his muscular stone thighs.
Moonlight edges across the empty lawn.

Taffeta whispers. Someone is staring through
The white ribs of the pergola. She stares
At a small garnet pulse that disappears
Steadily seaward. Ah, my dear, it is you.

But you are not alone. A gardener goes
Through the bone light about the dark estate.
He bows, and, cheerfully inebriate,
Admires the lunar ashes of a rose,

And sings to his imaginary loves.
Wait. You can hear him. The familiar notes
Drift toward the old moss-bottomed fishing boats:
"Happy the heart that thinks of no removes."

This is your nightmare. Those cold hands are yours.
The pain in the drunken singing is your pain.
Morning will taste of bitterness again.
The heart turns to a stone, but it endures.

THREE PROMPTERS FROM THE WINGS

for George and Mary Dimock

ATROPOS: OR, THE FUTURE

He rushed out of the temple
And for all his young good looks,
Excellence at wrestling,
High and manly pride,
The giddy world's own darling,
He thought of suicide.
(The facts are clear and simple
But are not found in books.)

Think how the young suppose
That any minute now
Some darkly beautiful
Stranger's leg or throat
Will speak out in the taut
Inflections of desire,
Will choose them, will allow
Each finger its own thought
And whatever it reaches for.
A vision without clothes
Tickles the genitalia
And makes blithe the heart.
But in this most of all
He was cut out for failure.

That morning smelled of hay.
But all that he found tempting
Was a high, weathered cliff.
Now at a subtle prompting
He hesitated. If
He ended down below
He had overcome the Fates;
The oracle was false;
The gods themselves were blind.

A fate he could contravene
Was certainly not Fate.
All lay in his power.
(How this came to his mind
No child of man can say.
The clear, rational light
Touches on less than half,
And "he who hesitates . . ."
For who could presume to know
The decisive, inward pulse
Of things?)
   After an hour
He rose to his full height,
The master of himself.

That morning smelled of hay,
The day was clear. A moisture
Cooled at the tips of leaves.
The fields were overlaid
With light. It was harvest time.
Three swallows appraised the day,
And bearing aloft their lives,
Sailed into a wild climb,
Then spilled across the pasture
Like water over tiles.
One could have seen for miles
The sun on a knife-blade.
And there he stood, the hero,
With a lascivious wind
Sliding across his chest,
(The sort of thing that women,
Who are fools the whole world over,
Would fondle and adore
And stand before undressed.)
But deep within his loins
A bitterness is set.
He is already blind.

The faceless powers summon
To their eternal sorrow
The handsome, bold, and vain,
And those dark things are met
At a place where three roads join.
They touch with an open sore
The lips that he shall kiss.
And some day men may call me,
Because I'm old and plain
And never had a lover,
The authoress of this.

CLOTHO: OR, THE PRESENT

Well, there he stands, surrounded
By all his kith and kin,
Townspeople and friends,
As the evidence rolls in,
And don't go telling me
The spectacle isn't silly.

A prince in low disguise,
Moving among the humble
With kingly purposes
Is an old, romantic posture,
And always popular.
He started on this career
By overthrowing Fate
(A splendid accomplishment,
And all done in an hour)
That crucial day at the temple
When the birds crossed over the pasture
As was said by my sister, here.
Which goes to show that an omen
Is a mere tissue of lies

To please the superstitious
And keep the masses content.
From this initial success
He moved on without pause
To outwit and subdue a vicious
Beast with lion's paws,
The wings of a great bird,
And the breasts and face of a woman.
This meant knowing no less
Than the universal state
Of man. Which is quite a lot.
(Construe this as you please.)

Now today an old abuse
Raises its head and festers
To the scandal and disease
Of all. He will weed it out
And cleanse the earth of it.
Clearly, if anyone could,
He can redeem these lands;
To doubt this would be absurd.
The finest faculties,
Courage and will and wit
He has patiently put to use
For Truth and the Common Good,
And lordly above the taunts
Of his enemies, there he stands,
The father of his sisters,
His daughters their own aunts.

Some sentimental fool
Invented the Tragic Muse.
She doesn't exist at all.
For human life is composed
In reasonably equal parts
Of triumph and chagrin,
And the parts are so hotly fused

As to seem a single thing.
This is true as well
Of wisdom and ignorance
And of happiness and pain:
Nothing is purely itself
But is linked with its antidote
In cold self-mockery—
A fact with which only those
Born with a Comic sense
Can learn to content themselves.
While heroes die to maintain
Some part of existence clean
And incontaminate.

Now take this fellow here
Who is about to find
The summit of his life
Founded upon disaster.
Lovers can learn as much
Every night in bed,
For whatever flesh can touch
Is never quite enough.
They know it is tempting fate
To hold out for perfect bliss.
And yet the whole world over
Blind men will choose as master
To lead them the most blind.
And some day men may call me,
Because I'm old and tough,
And never had a lover,
The instrument of this.

LACHESIS: OR, THE PAST

Well, now. You might suppose
There's nothing left to be said.

Outcast, corrupt and blind,
He knows it's night when an owl
Wakes up to hoot at the wise,
And the owl inside his head
Looks out of sightless eyes,
Answers, and sinks its toes
Into the soft and bloody
Center of his mind.

But miles and miles away
Suffers another man.
He was young, open-hearted,
Strong in mind and body
When all these things began.
Every blessed night
He attends the moonstruck owl,
Familiar of the witless,
And remembers a dark day,
A new-born baby's howl,
And an autumnal wetness.

The smallest sign of love
Is always an easy target
For the jealous and cynical.
Perhaps, indeed, they are right.
I leave it for you to say.
But to leave a little child,
Roped around the feet,
To the charities of a wolf
Was more than he could stomach.
He weighed this for an hour,
Then rose to his full height,
The master of himself.
And the last, clinching witness.
The great life he spared
He would return to punish
And punish himself as well.

But recently his woes
Are muted by the moon.
He no longer goes alone.
Thorns have befriended him,
And once he found his mother
Hiding under a stone.
She was fat, wet, and lame.
She said it was clever of him
To find her in the dark
But he always had been a wise one,
And warned him against snails.
And now his every word
Is free of all human hates
And human kindliness.
To be mad, as the world goes,
Is not the worst of fates.
(And please do not forget
There are those who find this comic.)

But what, you ask, of the hero?
(Ah well, I am very old
And they say I have a rambling
Or a devious sort of mind.)
At midnight and in rain
He advances without trembling
From sorrow unto sorrow
Toward a kind of light
The sun makes upon metal
Which perhaps even the blind
May secretly behold.
What the intelligence
Works out in pure delight
The body must learn in pain.
He has solved the Sphinx's riddle
In his own ligaments.

And now in a green place,
Holy and unknown,
He has taken off his clothes.
Dust in the sliding light
Swims and is gone. Fruit
Thickens. The listless cello
Of flies tuning in shadows
Wet bark and the silver click
Of water over stones
Are close about him where
He stands, an only witness
With no eyes in his face.
In spite of which he knows
Clear as he once had known,
Though bound both hand and foot,
The smell of mountain air
And an autumnal wetness.
And he sees, moreover,
Unfolding into the light
Three pairs of wings in flight,
Moving as water moves.
The strength, wisdom and bliss
Of their inhuman loves
They scatter near the temple.
And some day men may call me,
Because I'm old and simple
And never had a lover,
Responsible for this.

LIZARDS AND SNAKES

On the summer road that ran by our front porch
       Lizards and snakes came out to sun.
It was hot as a stove out there, enough to scorch
       A buzzard's foot. Still, it was fun
To lie in the dust and spy on them. Near but remote,
       They snoozed in the carriage ruts, a smile
In the set of the jaw, a fierce pulse in the throat
Working away like Jack Doyle's after he'd run the mile.

Aunt Martha had an unfair prejudice
       Against them (as well as being cold
Toward bats.) She was pretty inflexible in this,
       Being a spinster and all, and old.
So we used to slip them into her knitting box.
       In the evening she'd bring in things to mend
And a nice surprise would slide out from under the socks.
It broadened her life, as Joe said. Joe was my friend.

But we never did it again after the day
       Of the big wind when you could hear the trees
Creak like rockingchairs. She was looking away
       Off, and kept saying, "Sweet Jesus, please
Don't let him near me. He's as like as twins.
       He can crack us like lice with his fingernail.
I can see him plain as a pikestaff. Look how he grins
And swinges the scaly horror of his folded tail."

ADAM

Hath the rain a father? or who hath begotten the drops of dew?

"Adam, my child, my son,
These very words you hear
Compose the fish and starlight
Of your untroubled dream.
When you awake, my child,
It shall all come true.
Know that it was for you
That all things were begun."

Adam, my child, my son,
Thus spoke Our Father in heaven
To his first, fabled child,
The father of us all.
And I, your father, tell
The words over again
As innumerable men
From ancient times have done.

Tell them again in pain,
And to the empty air.
Where you are men speak
A different mother tongue.
Will you forget our games,
Our hide-and-seek and song?
Child, it will be long
Before I see you again.

Adam, there will be
Many hard hours,
As an old poem says,
Hours of loneliness.
I cannot ease them for you;
They are our common lot.
During them, like as not,
You will dream of me.

Adam

When you are crouched away
In a strange clothes closet
Hiding from one who's "It"
And the dark crowds in,
Do not be afraid—
O, if you can, believe
In a father's love
That you shall know some day.

Think of the summer rain
Or seedpearls of the mist;
Seeing the beaded leaf,
Try to remember me.
From far away
I send my blessing out
To circle the great globe.
It shall reach you yet.

THE ORIGIN OF CENTAURS

for Dimitri Hadzi

> *But to the girdle do the gods inherit,*
> *Beneath is all the fiend's.*   KING LEAR

This mild September mist recalls the soul
    To its own lust;
   On the enchanted lawn
It sees the iron top of the flagpole
    Sublimed away and gone
Into Parnassian regions beyond rust;
And would undo the body to less than dust.

Sundial and juniper have been dispelled
    Into thin air.
   The pale ghost of a leaf
Haunts those uncanny softnesses that felled
    And whitely brought to grief
The trees that only yesterday were there.
The soul recoils into its old despair,

Knowing that though the horizon is at hand,
    Twelve paltry feet
   Refuse to be traversed,
And form themselves before wherever you stand
    As if you were accursed;
While stones drift from the field, and the arbor-seat
Floats toward some *millefleurs* world of summer heat.

Yet from the void where the azalea bush
    Departed hence,
   Sadly the soul must hear
Twitter and cricket where should be all hush,
    And from the belvedere
A muffled grunt survives in evidence
That love must sweat under the weight of sense.

Or so once thought a man in a Greek mist—
      Who set aside
   The wine-cup and the wine,
And that deep fissure he alone had kissed,
    All circumscribing line,
Moved to the very edge in one swift stride
And took those shawls of nothing for his bride.

Was it the Goddess herself? Some dense embrace
      Closed like a bath
   Of love about his head;
Perfectly silent and without a face.
    Blindfolded on her bed,
He could see nothing but the aftermath:
Those powerful, clear hoofprints on the path.

THE VOW

In the third month, a sudden flow of blood.
The mirth of tabrets ceaseth, and the joy
Also of the harp. The frail image of God
Lay spilled and formless. Neither girl nor boy,
But yet blood of my blood, nearly my child.
         All that long day
Her pale face turned to the window's mild
         Featureless grey.

And for some nights she whimpered as she dreamed
The dead thing spoke, saying: "Do not recall
Pleasure at my conception. I am redeemed
From pain and sorrow. Mourn rather for all
Who breathlessly issue from the bone gates,
         The gates of horn,
For truly it is best of all the fates
         Not to be born.

"Mother, a child lay gasping for bare breath
On Christmas Eve when Santa Claus had set
Death in the stocking, and the lights of death
Flamed in the tree. O, if you can, forget
You were the child, turn to my father's lips
         Against the time
When his cold hand puts forth its fingertips
         Of jointed lime."

Doctors of Science, what is man that he
Should hope to come to a good end? *The best
Is not to have been born.* And could it be
That Jewish diligence and Irish jest
The consent of flesh and a midwinter storm
         Had reconciled,
Was yet too bold a mixture to inform
         A simple child?

Even as gold is tried, Gentile and Jew.
If that ghost was a girl's, I swear to it:
Your mother shall be far more blessed than you.
And if a boy's, I swear: The flames are lit
That shall refine us; they shall not destroy
      A living hair.
Your younger brothers shall confirm in joy
      This that I swear.

HEUREUX QUI, COMME ULYSSE,
A FAIT UN BEAU VOYAGE...

for Claire White

Great joy be to the sailor if he chart
The Odyssey or bear away the Fleece
Yet unto wisdom's laurel and the peace
Of his own kind come lastly to his start.
And when shall I, being migrant, bring my heart
Home to its plots of parsley, its proper earth,
Pot hooks, cow dung, black chimney bricks whose worth
I have not skill to honor in my art.

My home, my father's and grandfather's home.
Not the imperial porphyry of Rome
But slate is my true stone, slate is my blue.
And bluer the Loire is to my reckoning
Than Caesar's Tiber, and more nourishing
Than salt spray is the breathing of Anjou.

(AFTER DU BELLAY)

RITES AND CEREMONIES

I   THE ROOM

> Father, adonoi, author of all things,
> > of the three states,
> the soft light on the barn at dawn,
> > a wind that sings
> in the bracken, fire in iron grates,
> > the ram's horn,
> Furnisher, hinger of heaven, who bound
> > the lovely Pleaides,
> entered the perfect treasuries of the snow,
> > established the round
> course of the world, birth, death and disease
> > and caused to grow
> veins, brain, bones in me, to breathe and sing
> > fashioned me air,
> Lord, who, governing cloud and waterspout,
> > o my King,
> held me alive till this my forty-third year—
> > *in whom we doubt—*
> Who was that child of whom they tell
> > in lauds and threnes?
> whose holy name all shall pronounce
> > Emmanuel,
> which being interpreted means,
> > *"Gott mit uns"?*

I saw it on their belts. A young one, dead,
Left there on purpose to get us used to the sight
When we first moved in. Helmet spilled off, head
Blond and boyish and bloody. I was scared that night.
And the sign was there,
The sign of the child, the grave, worship and loss,
Gunpowder heavy as pollen in winter air,
An Iron Cross.

It is twenty years now, Father. I have come home.
But in the camps, one can look through a huge square
Window, like an aquarium, upon a room
The size of my livingroom filled with human hair.
Others have shoes, or valises
Made mostly of cardboard, which once contained
Pills, fresh diapers. This is one of the places
Never explained.

Out of one trainload, about five hundred in all,
Twenty the next morning were hopelessly insane.
And some there be that have no memorial,
That are perished as though they had never been.
Made into soap.
Who now remembers "The Singing Horses of Buchenwald"?
"Above all, the saving of lives," whispered the Pope.
Die Vögelein schweigen im Walde,

But for years the screaming continued, night and day,
And the little children were suffered to come along, too.
At night, Father, in the dark, when I pray,
I am there, I am there. I am pushed through
With the others to the strange room
Without windows; whitewashed walls, cement floor.
Millions, Father, millions have come to this pass,
Which a great church has voted to "deplore."

Are the vents in the ceiling, Father, to let the spirit depart?
We are crowded in here naked, female and male.
An old man is saying a prayer. And now we start
To panic, to claw at each other, to wail
As the rubber-edged door closes on chance and choice.
He is saying a prayer for all whom this room shall kill.
"I cried unto the Lord God with my voice,
And He has heard me out of His holy hill."

II   THE FIRE SERMON

Small paw tracks in the snow, eloquent of a passage
Neither seen nor heard. Over the timbered hill,
Turning at the fence, and under the crisp light of winter,
In blue shadows, trailing toward the town.
Beginning at the outposts, the foxtrot of death,
Silent and visible, slipped westward from the holy original
      east.
Even in "our sea" on a misty Easter
Ships were discovered adrift, heavy with pepper and tea,
The whole crew dead.

          Was it a judgment?

Among the heathen, the king of Tharsis, seeing
Such sudden slaughter of his people, began a journey to
      Avignon
With a great multitude of his nobles, to propose to the pope
That he become a Christian and be baptized,
Thinking that he might assuage the anger of God
Upon his people for their wicked unbelief.
But when he had journeyed twenty days,
He heard the pestilence had struck among the Christians
As among other peoples. So, turning in his tracks,
He travelled no farther, but hastened to return home.
The Christians, pursuing these people from behind,
Slew about seven thousand of them.

At the horse-trough, at dusk,
In the morning among the fishbaskets,
The soft print of the dancing-master's foot.

In Marseilles, one hundred and fifty Friars Minor.
In the region of Provence, three hundred and fifty-eight
Of the Friars Preachers died in Lent.

If it was a judgment, it struck home in the houses of
      penitence,
The meek and the faithful were in no wise spared.
Prayer and smoke were thought a protection.
Braziers smoldered all day on the papal floors.

During this same year, there was a great mortality
Of sheep everywhere in the kingdom;
In one place and in one pasture, more than five thousand
      sheep
Died and became so putrified
That neither beast nor bird wanted to touch them.
And the price of everything was cheap,
Because of the fear of death.

How could it be a judgment,
The children in convulsions, the sweating and stink,
And not enough living to bury the dead?
The shepherd had abandoned his sheep.

And presently it was found to be
Not a judgment.

The old town council had first to be deposed
And a new one elected, whose views agreed
With the will of the people. And a platform erected,
Not very high, perhaps only two inches above the tallest
      headstone,
But easy to view. And underneath it, concealed,
The excess lumber and nails, some logs, old brooms and
      straw,
Piled on the ancient graves. The preparations were hasty
But thorough, they were thorough.
A visitor to that town today is directed to
The Minster. The Facade, by Erwin von Steinbach,
Is justly the most admired part of the edifice
And presents a singularly happy union

Of the style of Northern France
With the perpendicular tendency
Peculiar to German cathedrals.
No signs of the platform are left, which in any case
Was outside the town walls.
But on that day, Saturday, February 14th,
The Sabbath, and dedicated to St. Valentine,
Everyone who was not too sick was down
To watch the ceremony. The clergy,
The new town council, the students
Of the university which later gave Goethe
His degree of Doctor of Laws.
For the evidence now was in: in Berne, under torture,
Two Jews had confessed to poisoning the wells.
Wherefore throughout Europe were these platforms erected,
Even as here in the city of Strasbourg,
And the Jews assembled upon them,
Children and all, and tied together with rope.

It is barren hereabout
And the wind is cold,
And the sound of prayer, clamor of curse and shout
Is blown past the sheepfold
Out of hearing.

The river worms through the snow plain
In kindless darks.
And man is born to sorrow and to pain
As surely as the sparks
Fly upward.

Father, among these many souls
Is there not one
Whom thou shalt pluck for love out of the coals?
Look, look, they have begun
To douse the rags.

O that thou shouldst give dust a tongue
To crie to thee,
And then not heare it crying! Who is strong
When the flame eats his knee?
O hear my prayer,

And let my cry come unto thee.
Hide not thy face.
Let there some child among us worthy be
Here to receive thy grace
And sheltering.

It is barren hereabout
And the wind is cold,
And the crack of fire, melting of prayer and shout
Is blown past the sheepfold
Out of hearing.

III   THE DREAM

The contemplation of horror is not edifying,
Neither does it strengthen the soul.
And the gentle serenity in the paintings of martyrs,
St. Lucy, bearing her eyes on a plate,
St. Cecilia, whose pipes were the pipes of plumbing
And whose music was live steam,
The gridiron tilting lightly against the sleeve of
St. Lawrence,
These, and others, bewilder and shame us.
Not all among us are of their kind.
Fear of our own imperfections,
Fear learned and inherited,
Fear shapes itself in dreams
Not more fantastic than the brute fact.

43

It is the first Saturday in Carnival.
There, in the Corso, homesick Du Bellay.
Yesterday it was acrobats, and a play
About Venetian magnificos, and in the interval
Bull-baiting, palm-reading, juggling, but today

The race. Observe how sad he appears to be:
Thinking perhaps of Anjou, the climbing grace
Of smoke from a neighbor's chimney, of a place
Slate-roofed and kindly. The vast majesty
Of Rome is lost on him. But not the embrace

Of the lovers. See, see young harlequins bent
On stealing kisses from their columbines.
Here are the *dolces*, here the inebriate wines
Before the seemly austerities of Lent.
The couples form tight-packed, irregular lines

On each side of the mile-long, gorgeous course.
The men have whips and sticks with bunting tied
About them. Anointed Folly and his bride
Ordain Misrule. Camel and Barbary horse
Shall feel the general mirth upon their hide.

First down the gantlet, twenty chosen asses,
Grey, Midas-eared, mild beasts receive the jeers
And clouts of the young crowd. Consort of brasses
Salutes the victor at the far end. Glasses
Are filled again, the men caress their dears,

The children shout. But who are these that stand
And shuffle shyly at the starting line?
Twenty young men, naked, except the band
Around their loins, wait for the horn's command.
Christ's Vicar chose them, and imposed his fine.

Du Bellay, poet, take no thought of them;
And yet they too are exiles, and have said
Through many generations, long since dead,
"*If I forget thee, O Jerusalem, . . .*"
Still, others have been scourged and buffeted

And worse. Think rather, if you must,
Of Piranesian, elegaic woes,
Rome's grand declensions, that all-but-speaking dust.
Or think of the young gallants and their lust.
Or wait for the next heat, the buffaloes.

IV   WORDS FOR THE DAY OF ATONEMENT

Merely to have survived is not an index of excellence,
Nor given the way things go,
Even of low cunning.
Yet I have seen the wicked in great power,
And spreading himself like a green bay tree.
And the good as if they had never been;
Their voices are blown away on the winter wind.
And again we wander the wilderness
For our transgressions
Which are confessed in the daily papers.

Except the Lord of hosts had left unto us
A very small remnant,
We should have been as Sodom,
We should have been like unto Gomorrah.
And to what purpose, as the darkness closes about
And the child screams in the jellied fire,
Had best be our present concern,
Here, in this wilderness of comfort
In which we dwell.
                    Shall we now consider
The suspicious postures of our virtue,

45

The deformed consequences of our love,
The painful issues of our mildest acts?
Shall we ask,
Where is there one
Mad, poor and betrayed enough to find
Forgiveness for us, saying,
"None does offend,
None, I say,
None"?

Listen, listen.
But the voices are blown away.

And yet, this light,
The work of thy fingers, . . .

The soul is thine, and the body is thy creation:
O have compassion on thy handiwork.
The soul is thine, and the body is thine:
O deal with us according to thy name.
We come before thee relying on thy name;
O deal with us according to thy name;
For the sake of the glory of thy name;
As the gracious and merciful God is thy name.
O Lord, for thy name's sake we plead,
Forgive us our sins, though they be very great.

It is winter as I write.
For miles the holy treasuries of snow
Sag the still world with white,
And all soft shapes are washed from top to toe
In pigeon-colored light.

Tree, bush and weed maintain
Their humbled, lovely postures all day through.
And darkly in the brain
The famous ancient questions gather: Who
Fathered the fathering rain

That falleth in the wilderness
Where no man is, wherein there is no man;
To satisfy the cress,
Knotweed and moonwort? And shall scan
Our old unlawfulness?

Who shall profess to understand
The diligence and purpose of the rose?
Yet deep as to some gland,
A promised odor, even among these snows,
Steals in like contraband.

Forgiven be the whole Congregation of the Children of Israel,
and the stranger dwelling in their midst. For all the people
have inadvertently sinned.

Father, I also pray
For those among us whom we know not, those
Dearest to thy grace,
The saved and saving remnant, the promised third,
Who in a later day
When we again are compassed about with foes,
Shall be for us a nail in thy holy place
There to abide according to thy word.

Neither shall the flame
Kindle upon them, nor the fire burn
A hair of them, for they
Shall be thy care when it shall come to pass,
And calling on thy name
In the hot kilns and ovens, they shall turn
To thee as it is prophesied, and say,
"He shall come down like rain upon mown grass."

A LETTER

I have been wondering
What you are thinking about, and by now suppose
It is certainly not me.
But the crocus is up, and the lark, and the blundering
Blood knows what it knows.
It talks to itself all night, like a sliding moonlit sea.

Of course, it is talking of you.
At dawn, where the ocean has netted its catch of lights,
The sun plants one lithe foot
On that spill of mirrors, but the blood goes worming
through
Its warm Arabian nights,
Naming your pounding name again in the dark heart-root.

Who shall, of course, be nameless.
Anyway, I should want you to know I have done my
best,
As I'm sure you have, too.
Others are bound to us, the gentle and blameless
Whose names are not confessed
In the ceaseless palaver. My dearest, the clear unquarried blue

Of those depths is all but blinding.
You may remember that once you brought my boys
Two little woolly birds.
Yesterday the older one asked for you upon finding
Your thrush among his toys.
And the tides welled about me, and I could find no words.

There is not much else to tell.
One tries one's best to continue as before,
Doing some little good.
But I would have you know that all is not well
With a man dead set to ignore
The endless repetitions of his own murmurous blood.

THE SEVEN DEADLY SINS

Wood engravings by Leonard Baskin

PRIDE

"For me Almighty God Himself has died,"
Said one who formerly rebuked his pride
With, "Father, I am not worthy," and here denied
The Mercy by which each of us is tried.

ENVY

When, to a popular tune, God's Mercy and Justice
    Coagulate here again,
Establishing in tissue the True Republic
    Of good looks to all men
And victuals and wit and the holy sloth of the lily,
    Thou shalt not toil nor spin.

WRATH

I saw in stalls of pearl the heavenly hosts,
  Gentle as down, and without private parts.
"Dies Irae," they sang, and I could smell
  The dead-white phosphorus of sacred hearts.

S L O T H

The first man leaps the ditch. (Who wins this race
      Wins laurel, but laurel dies.)
The next falls in (who in his hour of grace
      Plucked out his offending eyes.)
The blind still lead. (Consider the ant's ways;
      Consider, and be wise.)

AVARICE

The penniless Indian fakirs and their camels
Slip through the needle's eye
To bliss (for neither flesh nor spirit trammels
Such as are prone to die)
And from emaciate heaven they behold
Our sinful kings confer
Upon an infant huge tributes of gold
And frankincense and myrrh.

GLUTTONY

Let the poor look to themselves, for it is said
Their savior wouldn't turn stones into bread.
And let the sow continually say grace.
For moss shall build in the lung and leave no trace,
The glutton worm shall tunnel in the head
And eat the Word out of the parchment face.

L U S T

The Phoenix knows no lust, and Christ, our mother,
Suckles his children with his vintage blood.
Not to be such a One is to be other.

UPON THE DEATH OF
GEORGE SANTAYANA

Down every passage of the cloister hung
A dark wood cross on a white plaster wall;
But in the court were roses, not as tongue
Might have them, something of Christ's blood grown small,
But just as roses, and at three o'clock
Their essences, inseparably bouqueted,
Seemed more than Christ's last breath, and rose to mock
An elderly man for whom the Sisters prayed.

What heart can know itself? The Sibyl speaks
Mirthless and unbedizened things, but who
Can fathom her intent? Loving the Greeks,
He whispered to a nun who strove to woo
His spirit unto God by prayer and fast,
"Pray that I go to Limbo, if it please
Heaven to let my soul regard at last
Democritus, Plato and Socrates."

And so it was. The river, as foretold,
Ran darkly by; under his tongue he found
Coin for the passage; the ferry tossed and rolled;
The sages stood on their appointed ground,
Sighing, all as foretold. The mind was tasked;
He had not dreamed that so many had died.
"But where is Alcibiades," he asked,
"The golden roisterer, the animal pride?"

These sages who had spoken of the love
And enmity of things, how all things flow,
Stood in a light no life is witness of,
And Socrates, whose wisdom was to know
He did not know, spoke with a solemn mien,
And all his wonderful ugliness was lit,
"He whom I loved for what he might have been
Freezes with traitors in the ultimate pit."

BIRDWATCHERS OF AMERICA

I suffer now continually from ver-
tigo, and today, 23rd of January,
1862, I received a singular warning:
I felt the wind of the wing of mad-
ness pass over me.

BAUDELAIRE, *Journals*

It's all very well to dream of a dove that saves,
      Picasso's or the Pope's,
The one that annually coos in Our Lady's ear
      Half the world's hopes,
And the other one that shall cunningly engineer
The retirement of all businessmen to their graves,
      And when this is brought about
Make us the loving brothers of every lout—

But in our part of the country a false dusk
      Lingers for hours; it steams
From the soaked hay, wades in the cloudy woods,
      Engendering other dreams.
Formless and soft beyond the fence it broods
Or rises as a faint and rotten musk
      Out of a broken stalk.
There are some things of which we seldom talk;

For instance, the woman next door, whom we hear at night,
      Claims that when she was small
She found a man stone dead near the cedar trees
      After the first snowfall.
The air was clear. He seemed in ultimate peace
Except that he had no eyes. Rigid and bright
      Upon the forehead, furred
With a light frost, crouched an outrageous bird.

THE SONG OF THE FLEA

Beware of those that flatter;
Likewise beware of those
That would redress the matter
By publishing their woes.
They would corrupt your nature
For their own purposes
And taint God's every creature
With pestilent disease.

Now look you in the mirror
And swear to your own face
It never dealt in error
With pity or with praise.
Swear that there is no Circe,
And swear me, if you can,
That without aid or mercy
You are but your own man.

If you can swear thus nimbly
Then we can end our wars
And join in the assembly
Of jungle predators,
For honestly to thieve
Bespeaks a brotherhood:
Without a "by your leave"
I live upon your blood.

THE MAN WHO MARRIED MAGDALENE

Variation on a Theme by Louis Simpson

Then said the Lord, dost thou well to be angry?

I have been in this bar
For close to seven days.
The dark girl over there,
For a modest dollar, lays.

And you can get a blow-job
Where other men have pissed
In the little room that's sacred
To the Evangelist—

If you're inclined that way.
For myself, I drink and sleep.
The floor is knotty cedar
But the beer is flat and cheap.

And you can bet your life
I'll be here another seven.
Stranger, here's to my wife,
Who died and went to heaven.

She was a famous beauty,
But *our very breath is loaned.*
The rabbi's voice was fruity,
And since then I've been stoned—

A royal, nonstop bender.
But your money's no good here;
Put it away. Bartender,
Give my friend a beer.

I dreamed the other night
When the sky was full of stars
That I stood outside a gate
And looked in through the bars.

Two angels stood together.
A purple light was shed
From their every metal feather.
And then one of them said,

"It was pretty much the same
For years and years and years,
But since the Christians came
The place is full of queers.

Still, let them have their due.
Things here are far less solemn.
Instead of each beardy Jew
Muttering, 'Shalom, Shalom,'

There's a down-to-earth, informal
Fleshiness to the scene;
It's healthier, more normal,
If you know what I mean.

Such as once went to Gehenna
Now dance among the blessed.
But Mary Magdalena,
She had it the best."

And he nudged his feathered friend
And gave him a wicked leer,
And I woke up and fought back
The nausea with a beer.

What man shall understand
The Lord's mysterious way?
My tongue is thick with worship
And whiskey, and some day

I will come to in Bellevue
And make psalms unto the Lord.
But verily I tell you,
She hath her reward.

IMPROVISATIONS ON AESOP

1   It was a tortoise aspiring to fly
     That murdered Aeschylus. All men must die.

2   The crocodile rends man and beast to death
     And has St. Francis' birds to pick his teeth.

3   Lorenzo sponsored artists, and the ant
     Must save to give the grasshopper a grant.

4   The blind man bears the lame, who gives him eyes;
     Only the weak make common enterprise.

5   Frogs into bulls, sows' ears into silk purses,
     These are our hopes in youth, in age our curses.

6   Spare not the rod, lest thy child be undone,
     And at the gallows cry, "Behold thy son."

7   The Fox and Buddha put away their lust:
     "Sour grapes!" they cry, "All but the soul is dust!"

8   An ass may look at an angel, Balaam was shown;
     Cudgel they wits, and leave thine ass alone.

9   Is not that pastoral instruction sweet
     Which says who shall be eaten, who shall eat?

THE THOUGHTFUL ROISTERER DECLINES THE GAMBIT

I'm not going to get myself shot full of holes
For comparative strangers, like Richelieu or the King;
I prefer to investigate how a coward may cling
To the modest ways of simple civilian souls.
If I couldn't put down a little bit of the hair
Of the dog each day, I'd be as good as dead;
And it's nothing to me that a man will die in bed
Or under the table without the *Croix de Guerre*.

So as far as I'm concerned, you can drop the act
About the Immortal Fame and Illustrious End.
I shall die unsung, but with all of me intact,
Toasting His Noble Majesty and His Grace.
And if I die by the mouth, believe me, friend,
It won't be the cannon's mouth, in any case.

(AFTER CHARLES VION DE DALIBRAY)

GIANT TORTOISE

I am related to stones
The slow accretion of moss where dirt is wedged
Long waxy hair that can split boulders.
Events are not important.

I live in my bone
Recalling the hour of my death.
It takes more toughness than most have got.
Or a saintliness.

Strength of a certain kind, anyway.
Bald toothless clumsy perhaps
With all the indignity of old age
But age is not important.

There is nothing worth remembering
But the silver glint in the muck
The thickening of great trees
The hard crust getting harder.

"MORE LIGHT! MORE LIGHT!"

for Heinrich Blücher and Hannah Arendt

Composed in the Tower before his execution
These moving verses, and being brought at that time
Painfully to the stake, submitted, declaring thus:
"I implore my God to witness that I have made no crime."

Nor was he forsaken of courage, but the death was horrible,
The sack of gunpowder failing to ignite.
His legs were blistered sticks on which the black sap
Bubbled and burst as he howled for the Kindly Light.

And that was but one, and by no means one of the worst;
Permitted at least his pitiful dignity;
And such as were by made prayers in the name of Christ,
That shall judge all men, for his soul's tranquillity.

We move now to outside a German wood.
Three men are there commanded to dig a hole
In which the two Jews are ordered to lie down
And be buried alive by the third, who is a Pole.

Not light from the shrine at Weimar beyond the hill
Nor light from heaven appeared. But he did refuse.
A Lüger settled back deeply in its glove.
He was ordered to change places with the Jews.

Much casual death had drained away their souls.
The thick dirt mounted toward the quivering chin.
When only the head was exposed the order came
To dig him out again and to get back in.

No light, no light in the blue Polish eye.
When he finished a riding boot packed down the earth.
The Lüger hovered lightly in its glove.
He was shot in the belly and in three hours bled to death.

64

No prayers or incense rose up in those hours
Which grew to be years, and every day came mute
Ghosts from the ovens, sifting through crisp air,
And settled upon his eyes in a black soot.

"AND CAN YE SING BALULOO
WHEN THE BAIRN GREETS?"

All these years I have known of her despair.
"I was about to be happy when the abyss
  Opened its mouth. It was empty, except for this
  Yellowish sperm of horror that glistened there.

I tried so hard not to look as the thing grew fat
And pulsed in its bed of hair. I tried to think
Of Sister Marie Gerald, of our swaddled link
To the Lord of Hosts, the manger, and all of that.

None of it worked. And even the whip-lash wind,
To which I clung and begged to be blown away,
Didn't work. These eyes, that many have praised as gay,
Are the stale jellies of lust in which Adam sinned.

And nothing works. Sickened since God knows when,
Since early childhood when I first saw the horror,
I have spent hours alone before my mirror.
There is no cure for me in the world of men."

"IT OUT-HERODS HEROD.
PRAY YOU, AVOID IT."

Tonight my children hunch
Toward their Western, and are glad
As, with a Sunday punch,
The Good casts out the Bad.

And in their fairy tales
The warty giant and witch
Get sealed in doorless jails
And the match-girl strikes it rich.

I've made myself a drink.
The giant and witch are set
To bust out of the clink
When my children have gone to bed.

All frequencies are loud
With signals of despair;
In flash and morse they crowd
The rondure of the air.

For the wicked have grown strong,
Their numbers mock at death,
Their cow brings forth its young,
Their bull engendereth.

Their very fund of strength,
Satan, bestrides the globe;
He stalks its breadth and length
And finds out even Job.

Yet by quite other laws
My children make their case;
Half God, half Santa Claus,
But with my voice and face,

"It Out-Herods Herod. Pray you, avoid it."

A hero comes to save
The poorman, beggarman, thief,
And make the world behave
And put an end to grief.

And that their sleep be sound
I say this childermas
Who could not, at one time,
Have saved them from the gas.

FROM

A SUMMONING OF STONES

(1954)

DOUBLE SONNET

I recall everything, but more than all,
Words being nothing now, an ease that ever
Remembers her to my unfailing fever,
How she came forward to me, letting fall
Lamplight upon her dress till every small
Motion made visible seemed no mere endeavor
Of body to articulate its offer,
But more a grace won by the way from all
Striving in what is difficult, from all
Losses, so that she moved but to discover
A practice of the blood, as the gulls hover,
Winged with their life, above the harbor wall,
Tracing inflected silence in the tall
Air with a tilt of mastery and quiver
Against the light, as the light fell to favor
Her coming forth; this chiefly I recall.

It is a part of pride, guiding the hand
At the piano in the splash and passage
Of sacred dolphins, making numbers human
By sheer extravagance that can command
Pythagorean heavens to spell their message
Of some unlooked-for peace, out of the common;
Taking no thought at all that man and woman,
Lost in the trance of lamplight, felt the presage
Of the unbidden terror and bone hand
Of gracelessness, and the unspoken omen
That yet shall render all, by its first usage,
Speechless, inept, and totally unmanned.

LA CONDITION BOTANIQUE

Romans, rheumatic, gouty, came
To bathe in Ischian springs where water steamed,
Puffed and enlarged their bold imperial thoughts, and which
Later Madame Curie declared to be so rich
    In radioactive content as she deemed
        Should win them everlasting fame.

Scattered throughout their ice and snow
The Finns have built airtight cabins of log
Where they may lie, limp and entranced by the sedative purr
Of steam pipes, or torment themselves with flails of fir
    To stimulate the blood, and swill down grog,
        Setting the particles aglow.

Similarly the Turks, but know
Nothing of the more delicate thin sweat
Of plants, breathing their scented oxygen upon
Brooklyn's botanical gardens, roofed with glass and run
    So to the pleasure of each leafy pet,
        Manured, addressed in Latin, so

To its thermostatic happiness—
Spreading its green and innocence to the ground
Where pipes, like Satan masquerading as the snake,
Coil and uncoil their frightful liquid length, and make
    Gurglings of love mixed with a rumbling sound
        Of sharp intestinal distress—

So to its pleasure, as I said,
That each particular vegetable may thrive,
Early and late, as in the lot first given Man,
Sans interruption, as when Universal Pan
    Led on the Eternal Spring. The spears of chive,
        The sensitive plant, showing its dread,

The Mexican flytrap, that can knit
Its quilled jaws pitilessly, and would hurt
A fly with pleasure, leading Riley's life in bed
Of peat moss and of chemicals, and is thoughtfully fed
  Flies for the entrée, flies for the dessert,
    Fruit flies for fruit, and all of it

  Administered as by a wife—
  Lilith our lady, patroness of plants,
Who sings, *Lullay myn lykyng, myn owyn dere derlyng,*
Madrigals nightly to the spiny stalk in sterling
  Whole notes of admiration and romance—
    This, then, is what is called The Life.

  And we, like disinherited heirs,
  Old Adams, can inspect the void estate
At visiting hours: the unconditional garden spot,
The effortless innocence preserved, for God knows what,
  And think, as we depart by the toll gate:
    No one has lived here these five thousand years.

  Our world is turned on points, is whirled
  On wheels, Tibetan prayer wheels, French verb wheels,
The toothy wheels of progress, the terrible torque
Insisting, and in the sky, even above New York
  Rotate the marvelous four-fangled seals
    Ezekiel saw. The mother-of-pearled

  Home of the bachelor oyster lies
  Fondled in fluent shifts of bile and lime
As sunlight strikes the water, and it is of our world,
And will appear to us sometime where the finger is curled
  Between the frets upon a mandolin,
    Fancy cigar boxes, and eyes

Of ceremonial masks; and all
The places where Kilroy inscribed his name,
For instance, the ladies' rest room in the Gare du Nord,
The iron rump of Buddha, whose hallowed, hollowed core
    Admitted tourists once but all the same
    Housed a machine gun, and let fall

A killing fire from its eyes
During the war; and Polyphemus hurled
Tremendous rocks that stand today off Sicily's coast
Signed with the famous scrawl of our most travelled ghost;
    And all these various things are of our world.
    But what's become of Paradise?

Ah, it is lodged in glass, survives
In Brooklyn, like a throwback, out of style,
Like an incomprehensible veteran of the Grand
Army of the Republic in the reviewing stand
    Who sees young men in a mud-colored file
    March to the summit of their lives,

For glory, for their country, with the flag
Joining divergent stars of North and South
In one blue field of heaven, till they fall in blood
And are returned at last unto their native mud—
    The eyes weighed down with stones, the sometimes mouth
    Helpless to masticate or gag

Its old inheritance of earth.
In the sweat of they face shalt thou manage, said the Lord.
And we, old Adams, stare through the glass panes and wince,
Fearing to see the ancestral apple, pear, or quince,
    The delicacy of knowledge, the fleshed Word,
    The globe of wisdom that was worth

Our lives, or so our parents thought,
   And turn away to strengthen our poor breath
And body, keep the flesh rosy with hopeful dreams,
Peach-colored, practical, to decorate the bones, with schemes
   Of life insurance, Ice-Cream-After-Death,
      Hormone injections, against the *mort'*

   Saison, largely to babble praise
   Of Simeon Pyrites, patron saint
Of our Fools' Paradise, whose glittering effigy
Shines in God's normal sunlight till the blind men see
   Visions as permanent as artists paint:
      The body's firm, nothing decays

   Upon the heirloom set of bones
   In their gavotte. Yet we look through the glass
Where green lies ageless under snow-stacked roofs in steam-
Fitted apartments, and reflect how bud and stem
   Are wholly flesh, and the immaculate grass
      Does without buttressing of bones.

   In open field or public bed
   With ultraviolet help, man hopes to learn
The leafy secret, pay his most outstanding debt
To God in the salt and honesty of his sweat,
   And in his streaming face manly to earn
      His daily and all-nourishing bread.

JAPAN

It was a miniature country once
To my imagination; Home of the Short,
And also the academy of stunts
    Where acrobats are taught
  The famous secrets of the trade:
  To cycle in the big parade
While spinning plates upon their parasols,
Or somersaults that do not touch the ground,
    Or tossing seven balls
In Most Celestial Order round and round.

A child's quick sense of the ingenious stamped
All their invention: toys I used to get
At Christmastime, or the peculiar, cramped
    Look of their alphabet.
  Fragile and easily destroyed,
  Those little boats of celluloid
Driven by camphor round the bathroom sink,
And delicate the folded paper prize
    Which, dropped into a drink
Of water, grew up right before your eyes.

Now when we reached them it was with a sense
Sharpened for treachery compounding in their brains
Like mating weasels; our Intelligence
    Said: The Black Dragon reigns
  Secretly under yellow skin,
  Deeper than dyes of atabrine
And deadlier. The War Department said:
Remember you are Americans; forsake
    The wounded and the dead
At your own cost; remember Pearl and Wake.

And yet they bowed us in with ceremony,
Told us what brands of Sake were the best,
Explained their agriculture in a phony
    Dialect of the West,
  Meant vaguely to be understood
  As a shy sign of brotherhood
In the old human bondage to the facts
Of day-to-day existence. And like ants,
    Signaling tiny pacts
With their antennae, they would wave their hands.

At last we came to see them not as glib
Walkers of tightropes, worshipers of carp,
Nor yet a species out of Adam's rib
    Meant to preserve its warp
  In Cain's own image. They had learned
  That their tough eye-born goddess burned
Adoring fingers. They were very poor.
The holy mountain was not moved to speak.
    Wind at the paper door
Offered them snow out of its hollow peak.

Human endeavor clumsily betrays
Humanity. Their excrement served in this;
For, planting rice in water, they would raise
    Schistosomiasis
  Japonica, that enters through
  The pores into the avenue
And orbit of the blood, where it may foil
The heart and kill, or settle in the brain.
    This fruit of their nightsoil
Thrives in the skull, where it is called insane.

Japan

Now the quaint early image of Japan
That was so charming to me as a child
Seems like a bright design upon a fan,
    Of water rushing wild
  On rocks that can be folded up,
  A river which the wrist can stop
With a neat flip, revealing merely sticks
And silk of what had been a fan before,
    And like such winning tricks,
It shall be buried in excelsior.

LE MASSEUR DE MA SOEUR

I

My demoiselle, the cats are in the street,
Making a shrill cantata to their kind,
Accomplishing their furry, vigorous feat,
And I observe you shiver at it. You
Would rather have their little guts preserved
In the sweet excellence of a string quartet.
But, speaking for myself, I do not mind
This boisterous endeavor; it can do
Miracles for a lady who's unnerved
By the rude leanings of a family pet.

II

What Argus could not see was not worth seeing.
The fishy slime of his one hundred eyes
Shimmered all over his entire being
To lubricate his vision. A Voyeur
Of the first order, he would hardly blench
At the fine calculations of your dress.
Doubtless the moonlight or the liquor lies
Somewhere beneath this visible *bonheur*,
Yet I would freely translate from the French
The labials of such fleet happiness.

III

"If youth were all, our plush minority
Would lack no instrument to trick it out;
All cloth would emphasize it; not a bee
Could lecture us in offices of bliss.
Then all the appetites, arranged in rows,
Would dance cotillions absolute as ice
In high decorum rather than in rout."
He answered her, "Youth wants no emphasis,
But in extravagance of nature shows
A rigor more demanding than precise."

IV

"Pride is an illness rising out of pain,"
Said the ensnaffled Fiend who would not wince.
Does the neat corollary then obtain,
Humility comes burgeoning from pleasure?
Ah, masters, such a calculus is foul,
Of no more substance than a wasting cloud.
I cannot frame a logic to convince
Your honors of the urgent lawless measure
Of love, the which is neither fish nor fowl.
The meekest rise to tumble with the proud.

V

Goliath lies upon his back in Hell.
Out of his nostrils march a race of men,
Each with a little spear of hair; they yell,
"Attack the goat! O let us smite the goat!"
(An early German vision.) They are decked
With horns and beards and trappings of the brute
Capricorn, who remarked their origin.
Love, like a feather in a Roman throat,
Returned their suppers. They could not connect
Sentiment with a craving so acute.

VI

Those paragraphs most likely to arouse
Pear-shaped nuances to an ovoid brain,
Upstanding nipples under a sheer blouse,
Wink from the bold original, and keep
Their wicked parlance to confound the lewd
American, deftly obscured from sin
By the Fig-Leaf Edition of Montaigne.
But "summer nights were not devised for sleep,"
And who can cipher out, however shrewd,
The Man-in-the-Moon's microcephalic grin?

AS PLATO SAID

These public dances and other exercises of the
young maidens naked, in the sight of the young
men, were moreover incentives to marriage; and
to use Plato's expression, drew them almost as
necessarily by the attraction of love as a geo-
metrical conclusion is drawn from the premises.   PLUTARCH

Although I do not not know your name, although
It was a silly dance you did with apple flowers
Bunched in your hands after the racing games,
My friends and I have spent these several hours
Watching. Although I do not know your name,
I saw the sun dress half of you with shadow, and I saw
The wind water your eyes as though with tears
Until they flashed like newly-pointed spears.
This afternoon there was a giant daw
Turning above us—though I put no trust
In all these flying omens, being just
A plain man and a warrior, like my friends—
Yet I am mastered by uncommon force
And made to think of you, although it blends
Not with my humor, or the businesses
Of soldiering. I have seen a horse
Moving with more economy, and know
Armor is surer than a girl's promises.
But it is a compelling kind of law
Puts your design before me, even though
I put no faith or fancy in that daw
Turning above us. There's some rigor here,
More than in nature's daily masterpiece
That brings for us, with absolute and clear
Insistence, worms from their midnight soil,
Ungodly honk and trumpeting of geese
In the early morning, and at last the toil
Of soldiering. This is a simple code,
Far simpler than Lycurgus has set down.

The sheep come out of the hills, the sheep come down
When it rains, or gather under a tree,
And in the damp they stink most heartily.
Yet the hills are not so tough but they will yield
Brass for the kitchen, and the soft wet hair
Of the sheep will occupy some fingers. In the bottom fields
The herd's deposit shall assist the spring
Out of the earth and up into the air.
No. There is not a more unbending thing
In nature. It is an order that shall find
You out. There's not a season or a bird can bring
You to my senses or so harness me
To my intention. Let the Helots mind
The barley fields, lest they should see a daw
Turning to perch on some adjacent tree
And fancy it their sovereign ruler. No.
However we are governed, it shall draw
Both of us to its own conclusion, though
I do not even know you by your name.

DISCOURSE CONCERNING TEMPTATION

Though learned men have been at some dispute
Touching the taste and color, nature, name
And properties of the Original Fruit,
The bees that in midsummer congress swarm
In futile search of apple blossoms can
Testify to a sweetness such as man
Fears in his freezing heart, yet it could warm
Winter away, and redden the cheek with shame.

There was a gentleman of severest taste
Who won from wickedness by consummate strife
A sensibility suitable to his chaste
Formula. He found the world too lavish.
Temptation was his constant, intimate foe,
Constantly to be overcome by force, and so
His formula (fearing lest the world ravish
His senses) applied the rigors of art to life.

But in recurrent dreams saw himself dead,
Mourned by chrysanthemums that walked about,
Each bending over him its massive head
And weeping on him such sweet tender tears
That as each drop spattered upon his limbs
Green plant life blossomed in that place. For hymns
Marking his mean demise, his frigid ears
Perceived the belch of frogs, low and devout.

The problem is not simple. In Guadeloupe
The fer-de-lance displays his ugly trait
Deep in the sweaty undergrowth where droop
Pears of a kind not tasted, where depend
Strange apples, in the shade of *Les Mamelles*.
The place is neither Paradise nor Hell,
But of their divers attributes a blend:
It is man's brief and natural estate.

SAMUEL SEWALL

Samuel Sewall, in a world of wigs,
Flouted opinion in his personal hair;
For foppery he gave not any figs,
But in his right and honor took the air.

Thus in his naked style, though well attired,
He went forth in the city, or paid court
To Madam Winthrop, whom he much admired,
Most godly, but yet liberal with the port.

And all the town admired for two full years
His excellent address, his gifts of fruit,
Her gracious ways and delicate white ears,
And held the course of nature absolute.

But yet she bade him suffer a peruke,
"That One be not distinguished from the All";
Delivered of herself this stern rebuke
Framed in the resonant language of St. Paul.

"Madam," he answered her, "I have a Friend
Furnishes me with hair out of His strength,
And He requires only I attend
Unto His charity and to its length."

And all the town was witness to his trust:
On Monday he walked out with the Widow Gibbs,
A pious lady of charm and notable bust,
Whose heart beat tolerably beneath her ribs.

On Saturday he wrote proposing marriage,
And closed, imploring that she be not cruel,
"Your favorable answer will oblige,
Madam, your humble servant, Samuel Sewall."

DRINKING SONG

A toast to that lady over the fireplace
Who wears a snood of pearls. Her eyes are turned
Away from the posterity that loosed
Drunken invaders to the living room,
Toppled the convent bell-tower, and burned
The sniper-ridden outhouses. The face
Of Beatrice d'Este, reproduced
In color, offers a profile to this dark,
Hand-carved interior. High German gloom
Flinches before our boots upon the desk
Where the *Ortsgruppenführer* used to park
His sovereign person. Not a week ago
The women of this house went down among
The stacked-up kindling wood, the picturesque,
Darkening etchings of Vesuvius,
Piled mattresses upon themselves, and shook,
And prayed to God in their guttural native tongue
For mercy, forgiveness, and the death of us.

We are indeed diminished.
                          We are twelve.
But have recaptured a sufficiency
Of France's cognac; and it shall be well,
Given sufficient time, if we can down
Half of it, being as we are, reduced.
Five dead in the pasture, yet they loom
As thirstily as ever. Are recalled
By daring wagers to this living room:
"I'll be around to leak over your grave."

And *Durendal*, my only *Durendal*,
Thou hast preserved me better than a sword;
Rest in the enemy umbrella stand
While that I measure out another drink.
I am beholden to thee, by this hand,
This measuring hand. We are beholden all.

A POEM FOR JULIA

Held in her hand of "almost flawless skin"
A small sprig of Sweet William as a badge
Of beauty, and the region of her nose
Seemed to be made so delicate and thin,
Light of the sun might touch the cartilage
With numerous golden tones and hints of rose
If she but turned to the window now to smell
The lilacs and the undulant green lawn,
Trim as a golf course, where a haze revealed
The sheep, distinguished each with a separate bell,
Grazing and moping near the neighbor field
Where all the clover-seeking bees were gone,
But stood in modesty in the full sight
Of Memling, whose accomplished busy hand
Rendered this wimpled lady in such white
Untinted beauty, that she seems to stand
Even as gently to our present gaze
As she had stood there in her breathing days.

Seeing this painting, I am put in mind
Of many a freakish harridan and clown
Who by their native clumsiness or fate
Won for themselves astonishing renown
And stand amongst us even to this date
Since art and history were so inclined:
Here, in a generous Italian scene,
A pimpled, chinless shepherd, whose rough thought
And customary labor lead the ram
Into his sheep for profit and for sport,
Guide their ungainly pleasure with obscene
Mirth at the comedy of sire and dam
Till he has grossly married every ewe—
This shepherd, in a mangy cap of fur,
Stands at the window still regarding her,
That only lady, if the Pope speaks true,
Who with a grace more than we understand
Ate of her portion with a flawless hand.

And once a chattering agent of Pope Paul,
A small, foul-minded clergyman, stood by
To watch the aging Michelangelo
Set his *Last Judgment* on the papal wall,
And muttered thereupon that to his eye
It was a lewd and most indecent show
Of nakedness, not for a sacred place,
Fitted to whorehouse or to public bath;
At which the painter promptly drew his face
Horribly gripped, his face a fist of pain,
Amongst those fixed in God's eternal wrath,
And when the fool made motion to complain
He earned this solemn judgment of the Pope:
"Had art set you on Purgatory's Mount
Then had I done my utmost for your hope,
But Hell's fierce immolation takes no count
Of offices and prayers, for as you know,
From that place *nulla est redemptio.*"

And I recall certain ambassadors,
Cuffed all in ermine and with vests of mail
Who came their way into the town of Prague
Announced by horns, as history tells the tale,
To seek avoidances of future wars
And try the meaning of the Decalogue,
But whispers went about against their names.
And so it happened that a courtier-wit,
Hating their cause with an intemperate might,
Lauded his castle's vantage, and made claims
Upon their courtesy to visit it,
And having brought them to that famous height
To witness the whole streamed and timbered view
Of his ancestral property, and smell
His fine ancestral air, he pushed them through
The open-standing window, whence they fell,
Oh, in a manner worthy to be sung,
Full thirty feet into a pile of dung.

How many poets, with profoundest breath,
Have set their ladies up to spite the worm,
So that pale mistress or high-busted bawd
Could smile and spit into the eye of death
And dance into our midst all fleshed and firm
Despite she was most perishably flawed?
She lasts, but not in her own body's right,
Nor do we love her for her endless poise.
All of her beauty has become a part
Of neighboring beauty, and what could excite
High expectations among hopeful boys
Now leaves her to the nunnery of art.
And yet a searching discipline can keep
That eye still clear, as though in spite of Hell,
So that she seems as innocent as sheep
Where they still graze, denuded of their smell,
Where fool still writhes upon the chapel wall,
A shepherd stares, ambassadors still fall.

Adam and Eve knew such perfection once,
God's finger in the cloud, and on the ground
Nothing but springtime, nothing else at all.
But in our fallen state where the blood hunts
For blood, and rises at the hunting sound,
What do we know of lasting since the fall?
Who has not, in the oil and heat of youth,
Thought of the flourishing of the almond tree,
The grasshopper, and the failing of desire,
And thought his tongue might pierce the secrecy
Of the six-pointed starlight, and might choir
A secret-voweled, unutterable truth?
The heart is ramified with an old force
(Outlingering the blood, out of the sway
Of its own fleshy trap) that finds its source
Deep in the phosphorous waters of the bay,
Or in the wind, or pointing cedar tree,
Or its own ramfiied complexity.

CHRISTMAS IS COMING

Darkness is for the poor, and thorough cold,
As they go wandering the hills at night,
Gunning for enemies. Winter locks the lake;
The rocks are harder for it. What was grass
Is fossilized and brittle; it can hurt,
Being a torture to the kneeling knee,
And in the general pain of cold, it sticks
Particular pain where crawling is required.

> *Christmas is coming. The goose is getting fat.*
> *Please put a penny in the Old Man's hat.*

Where is the warmth of blood? The enemy
Has ears that can hear clearly in the cold,
Can hear the shattering of fossil grass,
Can hear the stiff cloth rub against itself,
Making a sound. Where is the blood? It lies
Locked in the limbs of some poor animal
In a diaspora of crimson ice.
The skin freezes to metal. One must crawl
Quietly in the dark. Where is the warmth?
The lamb has yielded up its fleece and warmth
And woolly life, but who shall taste of it?
Here on the ground one cannot see the stars.
The lamb is killed. *The goose is getting fat.*
A wind blows steadily against the trees,
And somewhere in the blackness they are black.
Yet crawling one encounters bits of string,
Pieces of foil left by the enemy.
(A rifle takes its temper from the cold.)
Where is the pain? The sense has frozen up,
And fingers cannot recognize the grass,
Cannot distinguish their own character,
Being blind with cold, being stiffened by the cold;
Must find out thistles to remember pain.
Keep to the frozen ground or else be killed.

Yet crawling one encounters in the dark
The frosty carcasses of birds, their feet
And wings all glazed. And still we crawl to learn
Where pain was lost, how to recover pain.
Reach for the brambles, crawl to them and reach,
Clutching for thorns, search carefully to feel
The point of thorns, life's crown, *the Old Man's hat.*
Yet quietly. Do not disturb the brambles.
Winter has taught the air to clarify
All noises, and the enemy can hear
Perfectly in the cold. Nothing but sound
Is known. Where is the warmth and pain?
Christmas is coming. Darkness is for the poor.

If you haven't got a penny, a ha'penny will do,
If you haven't got a ha'penny, God bless you.

IMITATION

Let men take note of her, touching her shyness,
How grace informs and presses the brocade
Wherein her benefits are whitely stayed,
And think all glittering enterprise, and highness
Of blood or deed were yet in something minus
Lacking the wide approval of her mouth,
And to betoken every man his drouth,
Drink, in her name, all tankards to their dryness.

Wanting her clear perfection, how may tongues
Manifest what no language understands?
Yet as her beauty evermore commands
Even the tanager with tiny lungs
To flush all silence, may she by these songs
Know it was love I looked for at her hands.

THE GARDENS OF THE VILLA D'ESTE

This is Italian. Here
Is cause for the undiminished bounce
Of sex, cause for the lark, the animal spirit
To rise, aerated, but not beyond our reach, to spread
Friction upon the air, cause to sing loud for the bed
Of jonquils, the linen bed, and established merit
Of love, and grandly to pronounce
Pleasure without peer.

Goddess, be with me now;
Commend my music to the woods.
There is no garden to the practiced gaze
Half so erotic: here the sixteenth century thew
Rose to its last perfection, this being chiefly due
To the provocative role the water plays.
Tumble and jump, the fountains' moods
Teach the world how.

But, ah, who ever saw
Finer proportion kept. The sum
Of intersecting limbs was something planned.
Ligorio, the laurel! Every turn and quirk
Weaves in this waving green and liquid world to work
Its formula, binding upon the gland,
Even as molecules succumb
To Avogadro's law.

The intricate mesh of trees,
Sagging beneath a lavender snow
Of wisteria, wired by creepers, perfectly knit
A plot to capture alive the migrant, tourist soul
In its corporeal home with all the deft control
And artifice of an Hephaestus' net.
Sunlight and branch rejoice to show
Sudden interstices.

92

The whole garden inclines
The flesh as water falls, to seek
For depth. Consider the top balustrade,
Where twinned stone harpies, with domed and virgin breasts,
Spurt from their nipples that no pulse or hand has pressed
Clear liquid arcs of benefice and aid
To the chief purpose. They are Greek
Versions of valentines

And spend themselves to fill
The celebrated flumes that skirt
The horseshoe stairs. Triumphant then to a sluice,
With Brownian movement down the giggling water drops
Past haunches, over ledges, out of mouths, and stops
In a still pool, but, by a plumber's ruse,
Rises again to laugh and squirt
At heaven, and is still

Busy descending. White
Ejaculations leap to teach
How fertile are these nozzles; the streams run
Góngora through the garden, channel themselves, and pass
To lily-padded ease, where insubordinate lass
And lad can cool their better parts, where sun
Heats them again to furnace pitch
To prove his law is light.

Marble the fish that puke
Eternally, marble the lips
Of gushing naiads, pleased to ridicule
Adonis, marble himself, and larger than life-sized,
Untouched by Venus, posthumously circumcised
Patron of Purity; and any fool
Who feels no flooding at the hips
These spendthrift stones rebuke.

It was in such a place
That Mozart's Figaro contrived
The totally expected. This is none
Of your French topiary, geometric works,
Based on God's rational, wrist-watch universe; here lurks
The wood louse, the night crawler, the homespun
Spider; here are they born and wived
And bedded, by God's grace.

Actually, it is real
The way the world is real: the horse
Must turn against the wind, and the deer feed
Against the wind, and finally the garden must allow
For the recalcitrant; a style can teach us how
To know the world in little where the weed
Has license, where by dint of force
D'Estes have set their seal.

Their spirit entertains.
And we are honorable guests
Come by imagination, come by night,
Hearing in the velure of darkness impish strings
Mincing Tartini, hearing the hidden whisperings:
"*Carissima*, the moon gives too much light,"
Though by its shining it invests
Her bodice with such gains

As show their shadowed worth
Deep in the cleavage. Lanterns, lamps
Of pumpkin-colored paper dwell upon
The implications of the skin-tight silk, allude
Directly to the body; under the subdued
Report of corks, whisperings, the *chaconne*,
Boisterous water runs its ramps
Out, to the end of mirth.

Accommodating plants
  Give umbrage where the lovers delve
 Deeply for love, give way to their delight,
As Pliny's pregnant mouse, bearing unborn within her
Lewd sons and pregnant daughters, hears the adept beginner:
  "*Cor mio*, your supports are much too tight,"
   While overhead the stars resolve
    Every extravagance.

  Tomorrow, before dawn,
   Gardeners will come to resurrect
 Downtrodden iris, dispose of broken glass,
Return the diamond earrings to the villa, but
As for the moss upon the statue's shoulder, not
  To defeat its green invasion, but to pass
   Over the liberal effect
    Caprice and cunning spawn.

  For thus it was designed:
   Controlled disorder at the heart
 Of everything, the paradox, the old
Oxymoronic itch to set the formal strictures
Within a natural context, where the tension lectures
  Us on our mortal state, and by controlled
   Disorder, labors to keep art
    From being too refined.

  Susan, it had been once
   My hope to see this place with you,
 See it as in the hour of thoughtless youth.
For age mocks all diversity, its genesis,
And whispers to the heart, "*Cor mio*, beyond all this
  Lies the unchangeable and abstract truth,"
   Claims of the grass, it is not true,
    And makes our youth its dunce.

Therefore, some later day
Recall these words, let them be read
Between us, let them signify that here
Are more than formulas, that age sees no more clearly
For its poor eyesight, and philosophy grows surly,
That falling water and the blood's career
Lead down the garden path to bed
And win us both to May.

A DEEP BREATH AT DAWN

Morning has come at last. The rational light
Discovers even the humblest thing that yearns
For heaven; from its scaled and shadeless height,
Figures its difficult way among the ferns,
Nests in the trees, and is ambitious to warm
The chilled vein, and to light the spider's thread
With modulations hastening to a storm
Of the full spectrum, rushing from red to red.
I have watched its refinements since the dawn,
When, at the birdcall, all the ghosts were gone.

The wolf, the fig tree, and the woodpecker
Were sacred once to Undertaker Mars;
Honor was done in Rome to that home-wrecker
Whose armor and whose ancient, toughened scars
Made dance the very meat of Venus' heart,
And hot her ichor, and immense her eyes,
Till his rough ways and her invincible art
Locked and laid low their shining, tangled thighs.
My garden yields his fig tree, even now
Bearing heraldic fruit at every bough.

Someone I have not seen for six full years
Might pass this garden through, and might pass by
The oleander bush, the bitter pears
Unfinished by the sun, with only an eye
For the sun-speckled shade of the fig tree,
And shelter in its gloom, and raise his hand
For tribute and for nourishment (for he
Was once entirely at the god's command)
But that his nature, being all undone,
Cannot abide the clarity of the sun.

Morning deceived him those six years ago.
Morning swam in the pasture, being all green
And yellow, and the swallow coiled in slow
Passage of dials and spires above the scene
Cluttered with dandelions, near the fence
Where the hens strutted redheaded and wreathed
With dark, imponderable chicken sense,
Hardly two hundred yards from where he breathed,
And where, from their declamatory roosts,
The cocks cried brazenly against all ghosts.

Warmth in the milling air, the warmth of blood;
The dampness of the earth; the forest floor
Of fallen needles, the dried and creviced mud,
Lay matted and caked with sunlight, and the war
Seemed elsewhere; light impeccable, unmixed,
Made accurate the swallow's traveling print
Over the pasture, till he saw it fixed
Perfectly on a little patch of mint.
And he could feel in his body, driven home,
The wild tooth of the wolf that suckled Rome.

What if he came and stood beside my tree,
A poor, transparent thing with nothing to do,
His chest showing a jagged vacancy
Through which I might admire the distant view?
My house is solid, and the windows house
In their fine membranes the gelatinous light,
But darkness follows, and the dark allows
Obscure hints of a tapping sound at night.
And yet it may be merely that I dream
A woodpecker attacks the attic beam.

It is as well the light keeps him away;
We should have little to say in days like these,
Although once friends. We should have little to say,
But that there will be much planting of fig trees,
And Venus shall be clad in the prim leaf,
And turn a solitary. And her god, forgot,
Cast by that emblem out, shall spend his grief
Upon us. In that day the fruit shall rot
Unharvested. Then shall the sullen god
Perform his mindless fury in our blood.

A ROMAN HOLIDAY

I write from Rome. Last year, the Holy Year,
The flock was belled, and pilgrims came to see
How milkweed mocked the buried engineer,
Wedging between his marble works, where free
And famished went the lions forth to tear
A living meal from the offending knee,
And where, on pagan ground, turned to our good,
Santa Maria sopra Minerva stood.

And came to see where Caesar Augustus turned
Brick into marble, thus to celebrate
Apollo's Peace, that lately had been learned,
And where the Rock that bears the Church's weight,
Crucified Peter, raised his eyes and yearned
For final sight of heavenly estate,
But saw ungainly huge above his head
Our stony base to which the flesh is wed.

And see the wealthy, terraced Palatine,
Where once the unknown god or goddess ruled
In mystery and silence, whose divine
Name has been lost or hidden from the fooled,
Daydreaming employee who guards the shrine
And has forgotten how men have been schooled
To hide the Hebrew Vowels, that craft or sin
Might not pronounce their sacred origin.

And has forgot that on the temple floor
Once was a Vestal Virgin overcome
Even by muscle of the god of war,
And ran full of unearthly passion home,
Being made divinity's elected whore
And fertile with the twins that founded Rome.
Columns are down. Unknown the ruined face
Of travertine, found in a swampy place.

Yet there was wisdom even then that said,
Nothing endures at last but only One;
Sands shift in the wind, petals are shed,
Eternal cities also are undone;
Informed the living and the pious dead
That there is no new thing under the sun,
Nor can the best ambition come to good
When it is founded on a brother's blood.

I write from Rome. It is late afternoon
Nearing the Christmas season. Blooded light
Floods through the Colosseum, where platoon
And phalanx of the Lord slaved for the might
Of Titus' pleasure. Blood repeats its tune
Loudly against my eardrums as I write,
And recollects what they were made to pay
Who out of worship put their swords away.

The bells declare it. "Crime is at the base,"
Rings in the belfry where the blood is choired.
Crime stares from the unknown, ruined face,
And the cold wind, endless and wrath-inspired,
Cries out for judgment in a swampy place
As darkness claims the trees. "Blood is required,
And it shall fall," below the Seven Hills
The blood of Remus whispers out of wells.

ALCESTE IN THE WILDERNESS

Non, je ne puis souffrir cette lâche méthode
Qu'affectent la plupart de vos gens à la mode . . .
MOLIERE: *Le Misanthrope*

Evening is clogged with gnats as the light fails,
And branches bloom with gold and copper screams
Of birds with figured and sought-after tails
To plume a lady's gear; the motet wails
Through Africa upon dissimilar themes.

A little snuffbox whereon Daphnis sings
In pale enamels, touching love's defeat,
Calls up the color of her underthings
And plays upon the taut memorial strings,
Trailing her laces down into this heat.

One day he found, topped with a smutty grin,
The small corpse of a monkey, partly eaten.
Force of the sun had split the bluish skin,
Which, by their questioning and entering in,
A swarm of bees had been concerned to sweeten.

He could distill no essence out of this.
That yellow majesty and molten light
Should bless this carcass with a sticky kiss
Argued a brute and filthy emphasis.
The half-moons of the fingernails were white,

And where the nostrils opened on the skies,
Issuing to the sinus, where the ant
Crawled swiftly down to undermine the eyes
Of cloudy aspic, nothing could disguise
How terribly the thing looked like Philinte.

Will-o'-the-wisp, on the scum-laden water,
Burns in the night, a gaseous deceiver,
In the pale shade of France's foremost daughter.
Heat gives his thinking cavity no quarter,
For he is burning with the monkey's fever.

Before the bees have diagrammed their comb
Within the skull, before summer has cracked
The back of Daphnis, naked, polychrome,
Versailles shall see the tempered exile home,
Peruked and stately for the final act.